My P

BY
DANA LYNSEY-GARTRELL

Tate Publishing, LLC

"My Beloved" by Dana Lynsey-Gartrell

Published in the United States of America
by Tate Publishing, LLC
127 East Trade Center Terrace
Mustang, OK 73064
(888) 361–9473

ISBN: **1-59886-05-3-4**

Dedication

This is dedicated first and foremost to my husband, my children, and their respective mates. They watched me sometimes scramble, sometimes climb, often collapse—in hopelessness—as I struggled with the impact of breakdown and depression. Too often, it was only being dragged back from the edge of the cliff of mental illness that made life go on. My family clung to every thread of hope that they WOULD see the "me" they used to know. They helped me "pick up the pieces" of that person when I was incapable of doing so.

I would have done anything to spare my loved ones the stresses they have experienced. The overcoming of a complete lack of understanding of mental health issues while "under fire" has been an enormous stress. It has been a harsh and exhausting journey for all of us. What we learned is simply essential to safeguarding healthy living in a stressful world.

When I was first hospitalized, I was mute and could not eat. As I began to recover, the psychiatrist assured me that this could all be a bad memory. At this point, I doubted her sanity more than my own. She said that the medical profession held the knowledge and expertise to help me become "better than I ever was." The real question was whether I would go the distance to reach that restoration or settle for a halfway measure.

The journey back to restored brain function is like no other. We are only as human as our brains allow us to be. The flat lining of the brain as neurological connections fail is a more distressing and terrifying journey toward death than the physiological failure of the heart. Sadly to all but the trained eye, this slow approach to death can be all but indiscernible. Seven years and two hospitalizations later, we have walked out of this shadowy valley.

It is also important to me to dedicate this book with inexpressible gratitude to those doctors and nurses who choose to take on the responsibility of "duty of care" to their brothers and sisters on this planet. To give human dignity to someone who has become for all intents less than human is the most powerful gift I have ever been given. As our earth becomes more fragile, so do its complex and interwoven inhabitants. The need for informed, intelligent, and selfless care has never been greater. The need for us all to take on the commitment to "first, do no harm" is critical.

I also wish to dedicate this book to my parents. To my mother whose financial support made it possible—its fabric has been woven from threads of her health challenges and mine. And to my father—whose unfailing commitment to an unhurried view of life taught me to look for the depth of understanding in things I might otherwise miss—to check and recheck and check again before taking ill-conceived action.

Acknowledgement

My thanks to my husband are boundless. The facets of love reflected in this book are in the greatest part shaped by his "husbandry." He is a gifted teacher by profession, and during this dark period of our lives he has found limitless depths of love in being tirelessly remedial. He has carried me, inspired me, and challenged my shattered spirit and broken mind. Despite the darkness in some of the valleys where we have been, he has never failed to bring out the best of who and what I am. I hope that the insights we have found at the bottom of these darkest valleys can enrich his life in return.

I have experienced few more frightening moments in life than hearing the psychiatrist, whose skills twice saved my life, ask my husband, "How do you feel? Do you feel she is fully 'back'?" At that time, I had been through a period of muteness, compulsory hospitalization, horrendous mental distress, and was finally restored to a barely-functioning human being. My husband's reply set a benchmark for the rest of my recovery. Had the bar been set too low, this book would certainly never have become a reality. Had it been set too high, the result would probably have been the same. I would have crumbled under the stress of trying to "get myself better" instead of working realistically with the physiological realities of neurological collapse and recovery.

I would also like to acknowledge the gracious contribution of Dr. John Stott. His willingness to contribute the foreword to this book has given encouragement and clarity of purpose. I hope anyone experiencing a difficult place in his journey can be inspired to look for companions—perhaps in unexpected places!

Foreword

It was the philosopher-statesman Francis Bacon in the 17th century who said that God had written not one book but two—the book of his words (Scripture) and the book of his works (nature). And 200 years later, Darwin borrowed his saying for the flyleaf of *The Origin of Species.* Thus Bible study and nature study (two investigations into divine revelation) belong naturally together.

Dana gives us in her book a beautiful example of this combination. She shares with us her acute observations of a family of Mute Swans on a small river at the bottom of her garden, and she delights us with her splendid photographs of the parent birds and their eight cygnets. She intersperses her pictures of these graceful birds with appropriate comments and Scripture verses.

I am impressed by Dana's eye for beauty. I also admire her honesty in sharing with us her painful struggles to climb out of a deep dark depression. Her swans helped her to recover, not least, as she observed their caring behaviour. She calls them her companions on her journey.

JOHN STOTT
Easter 2005

Introduction

The potential causes of an episode of mental illness are not the subject of this book. They are, however, the catalyst for its existence.

A human being is a complex and fragile creature—as is the planet he inhabits. I can only "set out my stall" from the outset that I believe we are fearfully and wonderfully made by a Creator and Redeemer whose supreme love, intelligence, and nature sustains everything we are and do. If we choose to let Him, He also is the author and craftsman, shaping all we can become.

I was raised a "common" or "garden" Christian. Somehow, a random and chance beginning to all we appreciate as life doesn't seem to make sense. It seems more possible that a 747 could come into existence and fly its maiden voyage successfully with no designing presence or guiding hand.

This book is not intended to change your view as to how our world came into existence. I hope you'll enjoy taking a journey through part of it with me. When we consider snapshots of nature as God's illustrations of His own Book, it illuminates a powerful story of love and purpose.

Leveled by depression, to a subhuman existence, I believed life was over as

I knew it, forever. The skills and knowledge of psychiatric treatment were applied with the sensitivity, wisdom, and dignity of those who dedicate their lives to such care. These individuals are truly unsung heroes. Like paramedics, their jobs are to extricate themselves from one's life at the earliest possible moment.

Humanity always teeters on the edge of exploiting the vulnerable. The humanitarian focus of these professionals' skills means that, unlike ages past, they are committed to dignity and security for those who have lost the ability to protect themselves. They are also wonderfully committed to restoring their fellow human beings to the autonomous state that makes that care superfluous. Before there is time for a restored, mind to say "thank you," they are gone. When I returned to the hospital to thank one of my medical carers, she smiled and said, "Its just what we do." What an understatement!

I believe we stand on the brink of a precipice in human understanding. Many choose to believe we evolved. Perceiving humanity as the pinnacle of evolution, we can, as technology makes it possible, assume a right to dismantle and manipulate everything around us—including the wonders of ourselves. Conversely, we can choose to retain a dignity and sense of sacredness at the awesomeness of ourselves. We are unique in all of creation. The concept that we are created in the image and likeness of a Creator who defines Himself and all His power as Love, gives us much to explore, hope for, and share.

This has practical and urgent implications for the world as we know it. The sovereign right of a human mind to form, inhabit, and wander its own neural pathways is something we all take for granted. As the secrets of unlocking those invisible worlds are revealed, they will also be subject to manipulation—potentially frightening manipulations of chemicals and electricity—of ever-greater precision.

Without understanding a Creator who created only good, man and his choices become a volatile mixture of good and evil. To the good, I owe my life, my mind, my ability to put these words on paper rather than banging my head mindlessly on a bookshelf because everything inside it seemed to have turned to jelly. To the potential for evil of man against man, I ask that we each consider how precious we are as human beings. We are unique among the creatures on our planet in our capacity to make choices. We are aware of that capacity of free choice, and we exercise it in contrast to limitations of instinctive behaviour. We will collectively sign over a God-given individuality if we neglect to take responsibility for our own humanity and all that means.

I believe we sell ourselves as a species horribly short when we feel we must accept a theory that says we can only return to a guttural cave-dwelling reality to understand who we really are. In a Biblical view, we return to a garden in a place called Eden. Accepting the good about ourselves and our fellow man, which has never diminished, we can seek to understand how and where evil was introduced into the equation. We can then begin to grasp the enormity of the gift of life we have been given and how to best live out good and minimize evil in our treatment of our fellow man.

The World Health Organisation predicts that mental distress will become the highest killer IN THE WORLD in less than twenty years, overtaking heart disease and cancer. It was with a critical sense of urgency that I needed to find the shortest route possible out of the depths of my own traumatized pit. I would urge us to challenge the concept of a capricious survival of the fittest as the explanation for the complexity of human life. Fundamentalist, self-imposed religious ignorance on the other hand is an equally flawed starting point. Both are ditches that can cause the wheels to come off when knowledgeable, caring skills are needed to aid humanity in travelling at the speed of light on the journey of life.

I would like to introduce you to some companions on my journey. In their own way, they, too, live at warp speed. A family of swans is raised to independence in a single year. As I watched our swan neighbors at work, I interacted with them and tried to capture their ethereal family life on film.

One of the hallmarks of deep depression is the speed at which processing spoken words becomes an exhausting and sometimes even painful experience. At my lowest points, my family would sometimes try to give me encouragement or insight. When I put my hands over my ears, in tears, and said "too many words," it was one of the darkest places in all of our lives. It was weeks before I could explain what happens when the human brain is depleted of the chemicals that fuel its processes. When precious words of encouragement become a dagger in the ear, the fear and confusion is overwhelming. The engine that fuels human reality is a delicate and marvellous machine.

I hope that through these photos and brief verses accompanying them, the swans can speak for themselves the powerful lessons of life and love.

"Ask the animals, and they will teach you. Ask the birds of the sky, and they will tell you. Speak to the earth, and it will instruct you. Let the fish of the sea speak to you. They all know that the Lord has done this. For the life of every living thing is in his hand, and the breath of all humanity."

~ The Story of Job ~

Job 12:7–10 (NLT)

Having suffered from a severe episode of depression, I experienced two stays in a psychiatric hospital. I was within a day of ECT. Recovery (whatever that was) seemed incomprehensible. ECT almost serves the function of CPR for the mind. The brain has gone to a place where pulling out of the depths of depression through its own resources is unreachable.

Medical expertise and the unfailing love and encouragement of my husband and children were life itself. I was incapable of returning that love with little but the response of a dry sponge to water. My daughter described my appearance later as "a walking ghost" and my mother described is as "a walking coma."

In one of countless acts of reassurance and affirmation, as I began the climb to recovery, my husband provided me with a digital camera. I relearned how to focus on moments in nature that I love so much: wind in the trees, the flow of running water, the harvests of the seasons, and the creatures I learned more about. Learning to use the camera required the reaffirmation of scrambled mental skills.

During this time, we lived in a house where a small river flowed at the bottom of the garden. Our neighbours were a pair of swans who made the river their home and raised two families of eight cygnets to maturity. Over time, they allowed me close enough to share the experience.

This little one is the offspring of that pair. The single-mindedness, dignity, compassion, selflessness, and courage these creatures pass on to a new generation year after year is awesome.

"God created … Every kind and species of flying birds.

God saw that it was good.

God blessed them: "Birds, reproduce on earth!"

~ The Book of Genesis ~
Genesis 1:20 (MSG)

Losing all ability to impact the world with meaning is a terrifying experience. When the chemical circuits in these brains of ours fail, the screen can go blank. It can also throw up some pretty weird and wonderful static. The expertise to aid the brain in its self-repair is a staggering feat that man has achieved.

That expertise promoted in me a steady and gradual return to human dignity. Although I was still severely limited in my ability to impact my world, taking photographs was a step on the way. I became an observer. My ability to finish the simplest tasks was limited—sometimes to a few minutes—before my head spun out of control again. If I was fortunate, I could say to my husband in frustration and desperation, "I have to rest—again."

The neural network that sustains our existence is something we take for granted every second of our conscious lives. Sometimes we can come to believe that we are the pinnacle of wisdom in the universe. We embrace an inaccurate view of our mortality.

I've learned that of itself, this is an unwise stance to take. We can miss so much. We can be oblivious to much. We can form such an inflated view of ourselves as human beings that we don't acknowledge or respect the creatures with which we share our globe. Yet it is we who threaten their ecosystems—not the other way around!

"God sets out the entire creation as a science classroom,

Using birds and beasts to teach wisdom."

~ The Story of Job ~
Job 35:11 (MSG)

My Beloved

When I first met our swan neighbours, I imagined I would spend a sunny hour taking a few photos. It was a therapeutic way of learning what the word "relax" meant.

As the seasons passed, I discovered that these beautiful, stately creatures have an intricate relationship with each other and their young. They can teach us many things. They challenge our values as mates and parents.

Mute swans are dynamic in their care for each other and their growing family. They display enormous wisdom and grace bringing their cygnets through a yearly cycle of maturity.

"Beloved, let us love one another, for love is from God . . ."

~ The First Letter of John ~
1 John 4:7 (NASB)

"Husbands, go all out in your love for your wives, exactly as Christ did for the church—a love marked by giving, not getting. Christ's love makes the church whole. His words evoke her beauty. Everything he does and says is designed to bring the best out of her, dressing her in dazzling white silk, radiant with holiness."

~ Paul's Letter to the Ephesians ~
Ephesians 5:25–27 (MSG)

Mute swans tend to stay together as pairs and raise new cygnets every year. Early spring is a wonderful renewal period of courtship where the male jealously guards the female and their territory. He watches over her, keeping between her and any other creatures that may approach.

Although these swans are called "mute," they have a variety of subtle verbal communications. From time to time, the male will show off to his female and anyone approaching. He rears up in the water, straightens his neck, flaps his enormous wings and calls in short, sharp barking noises. The message is clear: "This is MY beloved! No harm tolerated!"

"I am my beloved's and my beloved is mine . . ."

~ The Song of Songs ~

Song of Solomon 6:3 (NKJV)

". . . do this with humility and discipline—not in fits and starts, but steadily, pouring yourselves out for each other in acts of love, alert at noticing differences and quick at mending fences."

~ Paul's Letter to the Ephesians ~
Ephesians 4:2–3 (MSG)

"You were all called to travel on the same road and in the same direction, so stay together, both outwardly and inwardly. You have one Master, one faith, one baptism, one God and Father of all, who rules over all, works through all, and is present in all. Everything you are and think and do is permeated with Oneness."

~ Paul's Letter to the Ephesians ~
Ephesians 4:4–6 (MSG)

Swan pairs bond with each other in an elegant dance of gesture and response. Each is acutely aware of the movements the other makes. They are alert for anything that causes distress to the other. The male is quick to defend the female. In these photos, the male was patrolling the space between me and his mate. She quietly fed and groomed herself, swimming in his wake. Had I stepped several feet closer, I would have received a sharp warning hiss. Moving even closer would have provoked a warning display of flapping wings.

"What is your beloved more than another beloved . . ."

~ The Song of Songs ~

Song of Solomon 5:9 (NRSV)

›to was taken, this wonderful creature bit into a fishhook our shallow river. The mortality rate caused by swans ingesting discarded fishhooks is high.

‚k imbedded itself in the swan's beak. Every time he groomed ‚lf, he tore the skin on his back. Tinges of red streaked his beautiful white feathers.

By this time, the swans had a level of trust in me. They would feed out of my hand, let their babies feed from my hand, and often come when I called them. We requested an animal rescue officer to look at the swan. He was concerned that the swan would not survive many more days unless the hook could be removed. He tried several times to capture the swan with a rescue noose, but the swan would have none of it.

In desperation, I followed the swan along the water's edge. I knelt beside the bank and coaxed the swan toward me with bits of bread. I dropped the pieces closer and closer to my side until the swan was level with me. In one sudden movement, I fell sideways and tackled him, throwing my arms around his wings.

A threatened, full-grown swan is a fearsome sight. I could barely get my arms around his body to pin his wings flat against his sides. This calmed him, but each time I tried to readjust my grip, he dug the claws of his webbed feet into my bare legs.

Finally, I secured his wings and carried him to safety to have the fishhook removed. The female swam anxiously nearby. His muffled distress cries were like nothing I had ever heard, and I'm sure that it troubled her as well.

Once the rescue officer had removed the fishhook, we lowered the male into the river. Reunited with his beloved, the pair glided quietly into the evening shadows.

"My beloved speaks and says to me: "Arise, my love, my fair one, and come away; for now the winter is past, the rain is over and gone. The flowers appear on the earth; the time of singing has come . . ."

~ The Song of Songs ~
Song of Solomon 2:10–11 (NRSV)

This group of cygnets were very special to my husband and me. They appeared for their first river outing on the day my husband went into the hospital for major surgery. I took the photos to show him the new neighbors he would see when the surgery was over.

Once young cygnets arrive, the mother and father quickly adjust their roles. The mother swan is a fiercely devoted mother. She is constantly alert for danger, swimming in front of the cygnets and protecting them from any interference. The father and mother keep the cygnets between them patrolling the water around them.

"But we should behave like God's very own children, adopted into the bosom of his family, and calling to him, "Father, Father." For his Holy Spirit speaks to us deep in our hearts and tells us that we really are God's children."

~ Paul's Letter to the Romans ~
Romans 8:15 (MSG)

"Do not fear, greatly beloved, you are safe.

Be strong and courageous!"

~ The Words of Daniel ~

Daniel 10:19 (NRSV)

"This is my beloved and this is my friend . . ."

~ The Song of Songs ~

Song of Solomon 5:16 (NRSV)

Swans are selfless and tireless as they share the parenting roles. The little ones gain in strength and courage while both parents stand constant guard. Only when the cygnets are much larger and stronger will they be allowed to swim out of sight. Even then, they are never out of earshot. Their "peep-peep" murmurs assure their mother that all is well. The cygnets will be nearly adult size before their murmured calls begin to change to the "frrr-frrr" calls of the parents.

"Teach them to your children. Talk about them when you are at home and when you are away on a journey, when you are lying down and when you are getting up again. . . . so that as long as the sky remains above the earth, you and your children may flourish in the land . . ."

~ The Book of Deuteronomy ~
Deuteronomy 11:19 (NLT)

"As God's chosen ones, holy and beloved, clothe yourselves with compassion, kindness, humility, meekness, and patience."

~ *Paul's letter to the Colossians* ~

Colossians 3:12 (NRSV)

". . . my beloved brethren, let every man be swift to hear, slow to speak, slow to wrath"

~ The First Letter of James ~
James 1:19 (NRSV)

"But we must always give thanks to God for you, brothers and sisters beloved by the Lord, because God chose you as the first fruits for salvation through sanctification by the Spirit and through belief in the truth."

~ Paul's Second Letter to the Thessalonians ~
2nd Thessalonians 2:13 (NRSV)

Swan parenting does take patience. When the first cygnet is born, the father sometimes takes it for a "maiden voyage" while the mother is still waiting for the other eggs to hatch. It seemed to me that this first voyager determines that "he is going to be just like Dad."

In each of the three cygnet families we saw raised, one always acted as "trainee Dad." This robust, little ball of fluffy feathers would be first to chase off invading ducks or geese, first among his brothers and sisters to feed from my hand, and first to practice the intimidating hiss. It would be some time before his size and color matched his attitude, but the bravado was delightful to watch.

As the swans grow rapidly to maturity, their parents engage in a more energetic interchange with their little ones. A delicate balance between safety and independence is subtly altered as the cygnets mature. They are prepared for competent independence when the time comes.

"Everything we do, beloved, is for the sake of building you up."

~ Paul's Second Letter to the Corinthians ~
2nd Corinthians 12:19 (NRSV)

"You can tell for sure that you are now fully adopted as his own children because God sent the Spirit of his Son into our lives crying out, "Papa! Father!" "

~ Paul's Letter to the Galatians ~
Galatians 4:6 (MSG)

" . . . my beloved, be steadfast, immovable, always excelling in the work of the Lord, because you know that in the Lord your labour is not in vain."

~ Paul's First Letter to the Corinthians ~
1 Corinthians 15:58 (NRSV)

This display of spread feathers and arched wings has inspired many depictions of swans as symbols of dignity and beauty. It is also meant to be clearly understood. The parent swans use this show to let anyone near their babies know that they are on duty—a force to be reckoned with.

This warning presence with raised wings is the first sign that something has ventured too near. Until they are certain there is no threat to their little ones, they will maintain this posture. If the threat moves nearer, the male will lift himself out of the water and sweep toward the intruder.

"Guard me as the apple of your eye.

Hide me in the shadow of your wings"

~ A Psalm of David ~

Psalm17:8 (NLT)

"He will cover you with his feathers, and under his wings you will find refuge; his faithfulness will be your shield and rampart."

~ A Psalm of David ~
Psalm 91:4 (NIV)

"The beloved of the Lord rests in safety—the High God surrounds him all day long—the beloved rests between his shoulders."

~ The Book of Deuteronomy ~
Deuteronomy 33:12 (NIV)

The first time I saw all eight cygnets clamber up on their mother's back, I couldn't believe my eyes. I was certain that some had moved in front of her and out of my view. I wouldn't have thought it was possible for ALL eight of them to find shelter there at the same time.

Over the weeks, I saw them all repeatedly seek shelter simultaneously. As soon as the sense of threat passed, they all slipped quickly into the water for more exploration.

Human parents don't experience caring for so many babies at once. It was an inspiration to me to think that no matter how many of us run for cover in the shelter of God's wings, He has enough love and care for every need of every individual. There is room in the shelter of His wings for all mankind.

"But the eyes of the Lord are on those who fear him, on those whose hope is in his unfailing love, to deliver them from death and keep them alive in famine."

~ A Psalm of David ~
Psalm33:18–19 (NIV)

"Beloved, do not be surprised at the fiery ordeal that is taking place among you to test you, as though something strange were happening to you."

~ The First Letter of Peter ~
1st Peter 4:12 (NRSV)

Mute swans have a reputation for ferocious behavior when threatened. The male of each pair will fiercely guard the area where his cygnets are feeding. He will drive away any trespassers or threats. A full-grown male in a threatening posture will attack a human adult without hesitation.

I often sat on the edge of the river and fed the cygnets. As they gradually took their fill, their frantic "PEEP-PEEP" sounds would become quieter and less frequent. If the bread wasn't coming fast enough for their father's liking, he would step up on the bank and nip my foot.

On one occasion, he particularly felt I was derelict in my duty. He rose to his full height and hissed at me. Standing on the bank at full stretch, he was nearly looking me in the eye. Admittedly, it is a fearsome sight. We had a momentary stand-off. I stretched up on my toes and looked down at him and said—no! He looked puzzled for a moment and then lowered his neck. He nipped me once more on the toe as if to say—*Just don't forget this is serious business*—and then stepped back into the river.

". . . in my distress I cried out to the Lord; yes, I called to my God for help. He heard me from his sanctuary; my cry reached his ears. He opened the heavens and came down; dark storm clouds were beneath his feet. Mounted on a mighty angel, he flew, soaring on the wings of the wind."

~ The Second Book of Samuel ~
2nd Samuel 22:7–18 (NLT)

"Beloved, never avenge yourselves, but leave room for the wrath of God; for it is written, 'Vengeance is mine, I will repay, says the Lord.'"

~ Paul's Letter to the Romans ~
Romans 12:19 (NRSV)

"Have mercy on me, O God, have mercy on me, for in you my soul takes refuge. I will take refuge in the shadow of your wings until the disaster has passed."

~ A Psalm of David ~
Psalm 57:1 (NIV)

"Beloved, I pray that all may go well with you and that you may be in good health, just as it is well with your soul."

~ The Third Letter of John ~
3rd John 2 (NIV)

". . . but those who hope in the Lord will renew their strength. They will soar on wings like eagles; they will run and not grow weary, they will walk and not be faint."

~ The words of Isaiah ~
Isaiah 40:31 (NIV)

"Therefore, rid yourselves of all malice and all deceit, hypocrisy, envy, and slander of every kind. Like newborn babies, crave pure spiritual milk, so that by it you may grow up in your salvation, now that you have tasted that the Lord is good."

~ Peter's First Letter ~
1st Peter 2:1–3(NIV)

"I am not writing this to make you ashamed, but to admonish you as my beloved children."

~ Paul's First Letter to the Corinthians ~
I Corinthians 4:14 (NLT)

Out of the water, swans convey even more of their power and size. It is no small thing to be thrashed by an adult swan's wings.

One of "our" baby cygnets swallowed yet another fishhook. All that could be seen was the fishing line dangling from his beak. My neighbour and I knew that if we didn't catch him and take him to animal rescue, he would soon die.

She fed the swan family pieces of bread to keep them close to the bank. I stretched out on my stomach and fished the baby out of the water in a scooping gesture. His contented "peep-peep" turned to shrill cries. We had to persevere.

I tried to get back on my feet as quickly as I could. Before I could stand up at the edge of the river bank, I received a sound thumping around the head with powerful wings.

"All kinds of animals, birds, reptiles and creatures of the sea are being tamed and have been tamed by man, but no man can tame the tongue. It is a restless evil, full of deadly poison. With the tongue we praise our Lord and Father, and with it we curse men, who have been made in God's likeness."

~ The Letter of James ~
James 3:7–9 (NIV)

The story had a happy ending. I took the baby to the on-call veterinary surgeon who removed the fishhook safely. Wrapped in a towel and "peep-peeping" contentedly, we wandered the river together, until we found his family.

I had been told that swans will reject a cygnet touched by humans. As we approached the bank, the little one in my arms began to "peep-peep" with excitement. His mother left the group and moved toward the bank. I breathed a sigh of relief, but was still uncertain what would happen when he got near her.

I set him gently in the water and waited to see what would happen. Mama swam near him and bent over him, then she led him to the rest of the cygnets and "tail-end Charlie" took his place at the back of the group, safely surrounded by Mom and Dad. Each day the family came to the bottom of the garden, I counted eight little heads and smiled.

"Listen, my beloved brothers and sisters. Has not God chosen the poor in the world to be rich in faith . . ."

~ The First Letter of James ~

James 2:5 (NRSV)

"Consider the ravens: They do not sow or reap, they have no storeroom or barn; yet God feeds them. And how much more valuable you are than birds! Who of you by worrying can add a single hour to his life? Since you cannot do this very little thing, why do you worry about the rest?"

~ The Gospel of Luke ~
Luke 12:24–26 (NIV)

"How precious is your unfailing love, O God!
All humanity finds shelter in the shadow of your wings."

~ A Psalm of David ~
Psalm 36:7 (NLT)

"How great is your goodness, which you have stored up for those who fear you, which you bestow in the sight of men on those who take refuge in you. In the shelter of your presence you hide them from the intrigues of men; in your dwelling you keep them safe from accusing tongues."

~ A Psalm of David ~
Psalm 31:20 (NIV)

". . . you are mine. When you pass through the waters, I will be with you; and when you pass through the rivers, they will not sweep over you. . . ."

~ The Words of Isaiah ~
Isaiah 43:2 (NIV)

"For, all men are like grass, and all their glory is like the flowers of the field; the grass withers and the flowers fall, but the word of the Lord stands for ever. And this is the word that was preached to you."

~ Peter's First Letter ~
Ist Peter 1:24–25 (NIV)

"So teach us to count our days that we may gain a wise heart."

~ A Song of David ~
Psalm 90:12 (NRSV)

Watching the constant changes that occurred as the cygnets matured was an education all in itself. They grew from tiny little balls of fluff to almost full-sized young adults in less than a year.

Although they reach almost adult size, their grey colored feathers are slow to change. The patterns of dark and light grey alter with their size, providing perfect camouflage in the rippled water. It will be at least another year before they are fully mature and white.

"Beloved, since God loved us so much, we also ought to love one another."

~ The First Letter of John ~
Ist John 4:11(NIV)

The changes that take place in one year are amazing. Making room for each other on Mama's back is their first shared security.

As they mature, the cygnets will begin to share the burden of watchfulness and care. They practice hissing, chasing, imposing postures, quiet calls, and other skills they will need to nurture a next generation.

"Beloved, . . . with the Lord one day is like a thousand years, and a thousand years are like one day. The Lord is not slow about his promise, as some think of slowness, but is patient with you . . ."

~ The Second Letter of Peter ~
2nd Peter 3:8 (NRSV)

There are lessons embedded in creation that take time to appreciate. Sometimes the journey is as beautiful and enriching as the destination.

I never tire of taking close-ups of the wing patterns of maturing cygnets. As true white feathers begin to form, they form first underneath—completely hidden from sight. The fluffy, specked grey feathers form a dappled camouflage.

The sight of a full-grown cygnet with the last tiny specks of grey feathers on his neck and chest is a celebration. Another generation has reached maturity.

"Ask boldly, believingly, without a second thought. People who worry their prayers are like wind-whipped waves."

~ The Letter of James ~
James 1:6 (NIV)

"Therefore, my beloved, just as you have always obeyed me,
not only in my presence, but much more now in my absence,
work out your own salvation with fear and trembling;"

~ Paul's Letter to the Philippians ~
Philippians 2:12 (NRSV)

Some time before the following spring, most of the nearly mature cygnets will leave their father and mother's care. They will find other groups of swans. When they are fully mature, they will begin to seek their own mates and new generations will begin.

"My soul yearns, even faints, for the courts of the Lord; my heart and my flesh cry out for the living God. Even the sparrow has found a home, and the swallow a nest for herself, where she may have her young—a place near your altar, O Lord Almighty, my King and my God."

~ A Psalm of David ~
Psalm 84:3 (NIV)

Jesus Christ looked at the creatures He knew that had been formed "in the beginning." Foxes and birds had the homes He had created for them, but He had no permanent home during his adult life on earth.

It is a sobering thought. Were we to meet our Creator on earth, how would we respond . . . ?

"O Jerusalem, Jerusalem, you who kill the prophets and stone those sent to you, how often I have longed to gather your children together, as a hen gathers her chicks under her wings, but you were not willing."

~ The Account of Matthew ~
Matthew 23:37 (NIV)

"And now what are you waiting for? Get up, be baptised and wash your sins away, calling on his name."

~ The Acts of the Apostles ~
Acts 2:38 (MSG)

"But what happens when we live God's way? He brings gifts into our lives, much the same way that fruit appears in an orchard—things like affection for others, exuberance about life, serenity. We develop a willingness to stick with things, a sense of compassion in the heart, and a conviction that a basic holiness permeates things and people. We find ourselves involved in loyal commitments, not needing to force our way in life, able to marshal and direct our energies wisely."

~ Paul's Letter to the Galatians ~
Galatians 5:22–23 (MSG)

Belief in the myth of instant relationship is common in our world. We believe that somehow faster is always better. Swan pairs are commonly bonded together for life. Those whose bonds are not broken have a much higher success rate in parenting. Their young ones are given the greatest chance for survival. Learning and passing on the lessons of history applies even to instinctive creatures.

Brigitte Bardot is quoted as saying that "It is dreadful to grow old, but wonderful to ripen." In a few short years, these swans renewed my belief that we spend far too much time looking for instant solutions in life. It is only with time, care, and long-term commitment that we can truly grow in a depth of understanding and comprehension of others and ourselves that weathers all storms.

"May you be richly rewarded by the Lord, the God of Israel,

under whose wings you have come to take refuge."

~ The Story of Ruth ~
Ruth 2:12 (NIV)

"Are not two sparrows sold for a penny? Yet not one of them will fall to the ground apart from the will of your Father. And even the very hairs of your head are all numbered. So don't be afraid; you are worth more than many sparrows."

~ The Account of Matthew ~
Matthew 10:29–31 (NIV)

The terror and distress of complete mental breakdown is indescribable. I called out to God, but only heard my own words resonating emptily in my head. I tried to remember one of the hundreds of Bible verses I have read over the years. None of them gave comfort. For every one that gave comfort, another seemed to condemn. This is the nature of depression—hopeless downward spirals of negativity. In the midst of mental confusion and malfunction at every level, I was hopeless and convinced that I was close to death.

Sadly, the version of Christianity we give to others can reinforce hopelessness. We become preoccupied with finding failure rather than celebrating our Savior's sacrifice to cover ALL shortcomings. The one verse that gave me peace was the verse above. I could accept that God was aware of me and all I had become. If a sparrow couldn't escape his notice in falling to the ground, He surely would know where I was and what I had become. He could restore and renew.

As I recovered, this verse came to life even more. I studied the intricacy of a cygnet's maturing wing. God seems to have spent so much creative energy perfecting the ever-changing development of this tiny part of the enormity of creation. In a few short months this ever-changing protective artwork disappears forever. How much more must he be aware of the ever-changing neuron flows in this complex brain of ours.

"For the eyes of the Lord range throughout the earth to strengthen those whose hearts are fully committed to him . . ."

~ The Second Chronicle ~
2nd Chronicles 16:9 (NIV)

"This is how much God loved the world: He gave his Son, his one and only Son. And this is why: so that no one need be destroyed; by believing in him, anyone can have a whole and lasting life."

~ The Account of John ~
John 3:26 (MSG)

Only Jesus Christ has ever experienced the complete fullness of the journey from helpless babe to the fully matured and gloried Son of God. God was willing to give his precious Son to make that reality possible for us to share.
"He is the image of the invisible God, the firstborn over all creation."

Col 1:15 (NIV)

"Beloved, we are God's children now; what we will be has not yet been revealed. What we do know is this: when he is revealed, we will be like him, for we will see him as he is."

~ The First Letter of John ~

1st John 3:2 (NIV)

"I sent you Timothy, who is my beloved and faithful child in the Lord, to remind you of my ways in Christ Jesus"

~ Paul's First Letter to the Corinthians ~
1st Corinthians 4:17 (NRSV)

Until we do see him as He is we have much to experience in this unparalleled journey we call life.

"I have told you these things, so that in me you may have peace. In this world, you will have trouble. But take heart! I have overcome the world."

John 16:33 (NIV)

". . . my beloved every generous act of giving, with every perfect gift, is from above, coming down from the Father of lights, with whom there is no variation or shadow . . ."

~ The Letter of James ~
James 1:17 (NRSV)

Final thoughts:

I started this book by saying I believe in a Creator who gave us the supreme role in His creation.

He gifted us with intelligence, creativity, consciousness, and an unparalleled capacity to impact our world. With appreciation of these gifts comes great responsibility.

I learned how beautifully these swans instinctively live within their created capacities. When we as human beings live ours, we become aware of our Creator and are compelled to acknowledge Him.

It is awesome to discover the Artist behind the Art.

May God bless you in your discovery.

Dana

Help on the Journey

Severe clinical depression is a terrifying, disorienting place of mental, emotional, and physical distress. I understood nothing of the medical issues of depression while I was unable to comprehend them. My husband purchased a number of relevant books to help him understand what was happening to me. In my early recovery, it was impossible for me to even read the titles of those books, let alone grasp the information contained in them.

For a Christian, the same challenge exists in terms of the issues of faith. During a certain stage in mental illness, a great deal is irrelevant, confusing, and distorted in terms of the truths of salvation. The depressed human mind is like a vehicle running out of fuel. It coughs, it splutters, it stalls, it strains—every effort of thought is a struggle.

Issues of guilt and self-condemnation are part and parcel of the depressive experience no matter what the spiritual beliefs of the sufferer. The greys and blacks to which life is reduced fuel those perspectives. At that time, often inexperienced Christians can simply pour more fuel on an already tortuous fire.

My faith went through a complete meltdown. In the book of First Corinthians, Paul describes this refining spiritual process. What is not of eternal relevance and authenticity is simply burned away. In the throes of depression, this is an intensely terrifying experience. I became desperate for spiritual guidance that would strengthen and restore my foundation of faith in a way that held authentic relevance for myself, my husband, and my adult children who had all experienced challenges in our relationships with God.

I found the book "Contemporary Christianity" by John Stott. From its pages, the following quote spoke powerfully to me:

" . . . I have recently celebrated my seventieth birthday . . . at this age I do not expect to live much longer . . . So naturally I ask myself: Where are the Timothys of the next generation? Where are the young evangelical men and women, who are determined by God's grace to stand firm in the Scripture, refusing to be swept off their feet by the prevailing winds of fashion, who are resolved to continue in it, and live by it, relating the Word to the world in order to obey it, and who are committed to passing it on . . . ?"[1]

I have since read many books by John Stott and have found every one enlightening, strengthening, and completely focused on the big picture of Salvation. I would encourage anyone wishing to have a deeper understanding of these issues to turn to his writings as a starting point.

Endnote

I would wish to encourage anyone dealing with the physiological realities of mental trauma personally or in a loved one. A fruit of God's spirit needed through times of mental trauma is that of longsuffering. In the pruning and new growth, which only this kind of experience brings, the result is ultimately a blessing. Subsequent crops of goodness contain a larger yield of other more fully developed fruits. May God bless your increase.

(Footnotes)

[1] John Stott–The Contemporary Christian, p172 (1992) IVP

Contact author Dana Lynsey-Gartrell

or order more copies of this book at

TATE PUBLISHING, LLC

127 East Trade Center Terrace

Mustang, Oklahoma 73064

(888) 361 - 9473

Tate Publishing, LLC

www.tatepublishing.com